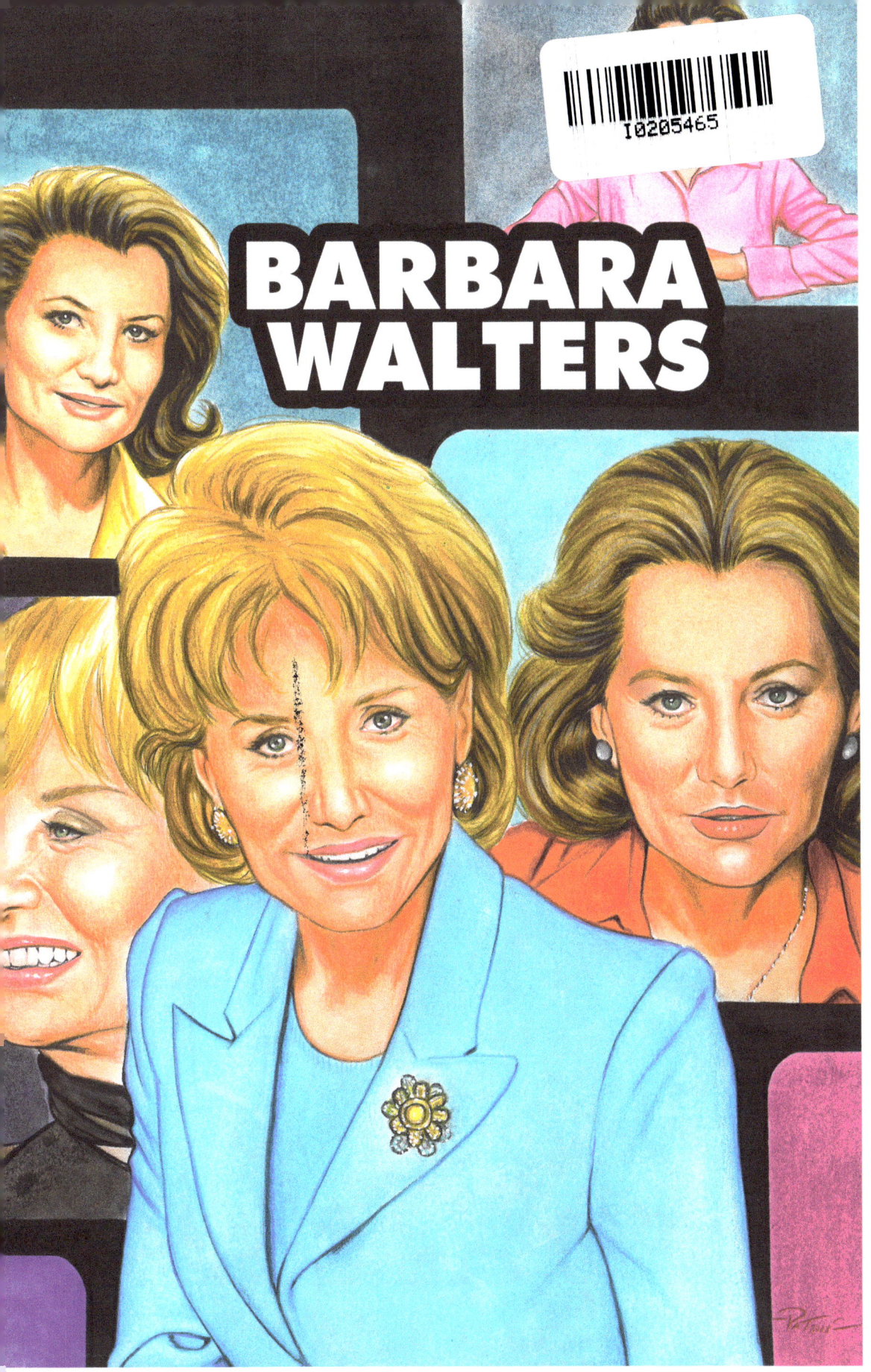
BARBARA WALTERS

BARBARA WALTERS WAS BORN ON SEPTEMBER 25, 1929 IN BOSTON, MASSACHUSETTS.

HER FATHER, LOU, WAS A NIGHTCLUB IMPRESARIO, KNOWN FOR PRODUCING LAVISH MUSICAL SHOWS UP AND DOWN THE EAST COAST. HE EVEN PRODUCE THE FAMED *ZIEGFELD FOLLIES*.

BARBARA HAS ALWAYS SAID THAT HANGING AROUND SO MANY GLAMOROUS STARS AS SUCH A YOUNG AGE MADE HER FEEL AT EASE AROUND FAMOUS PEOPLE.

AT HOME, IT WAS A DIFFERENT STORY.

BARBARA'S OLDER SISTER JACQUELINE WAS DEVELOPMENTALLY DISABLED. JACQUELINE'S CONDITION WAS A SOURCE OF EMBARRASSMENT FOR BARBARA. BUT IT ALSO TAUGHT HER HOW TO EMPATHIZE WITH OTHERS.

"ALL MY LIFE I HAVE FELT LIKE I WAS AUDITIONING," BARBARA LATER SAID. "I AUDITIONED FOR MY FRIENDS, I AUDITIONED BECAUSE MY SISTER WAS REJECTED."

ASIDE FROM THE COHN FIASCO, BARBARA SEEMED TO BE LIVING THE DREAM IN COLLEGE. BUT THERE WERE WARNING SIGNS AHEAD. IN HER YEARBOOK, SHE DEPICTED HERSELF IN A CARTOON AS AN OSTRICH WITH ITS HEAD IN THE SAND.

DID SHE HAVE A HINT OF WHAT WAS COMING NEXT? IN FLORIDA, SHORTLY AFTER GRADUATION, SHE MET AN ELIGIBLE BACHELOR, BUSINESS MAN BOB KATZ. THEIR RELATIONSHIP WOULD NOT END HAPPILY.

SMITTEN WITH HIS CATCH, JUST AS COHN HAD BEEN, BOB TOO PROPOSED MARRIAGE.

THIS TIME, BARBARA SAID YES.

THEY WERE MARRIED IN A LAVISH CEREMONY AT THE PLAZA HOTEL IN NEW YORK ON JUNE 21, 1955.

MILTON BERLE—MR. TELEVISION HIMSELF—WAS ONE OF THE GUESTS.

THERE WAS JUST ONE PROBLEM. BARBARA WASN'T INTERESTED IN PLAYING THE ROLE OF A WEALTHY BUSINESSMAN'S WIFE. THE STORK CLUB JUST WASN'T THE PLACE FOR HER.

AFTER JUST THREE YEARS OF MARRIAGE, THE UNION WAS QUIETLY ANNULLED.

THINGS SOON GOT EVEN WORSE. IN JUNE OF 1958, BARBARA'S FATHER TRIED TO COMMIT SUICIDE.

LOU WALTERS HAD FALLEN DEEPLY INTO DEBT AND WAS BEING HOUNDED BY THE IRS. THE GOVERNMENT PUT A LIEN ON THE FAMILY HOME IN FLORIDA.

TAX AGENTS EVEN TOOK THE CHANDELIER OFF THE DINING ROOM CEILING. FOR BARBARA AND HER FAMILY, THE GOOD TIMES WERE OFFICIALLY OVER.

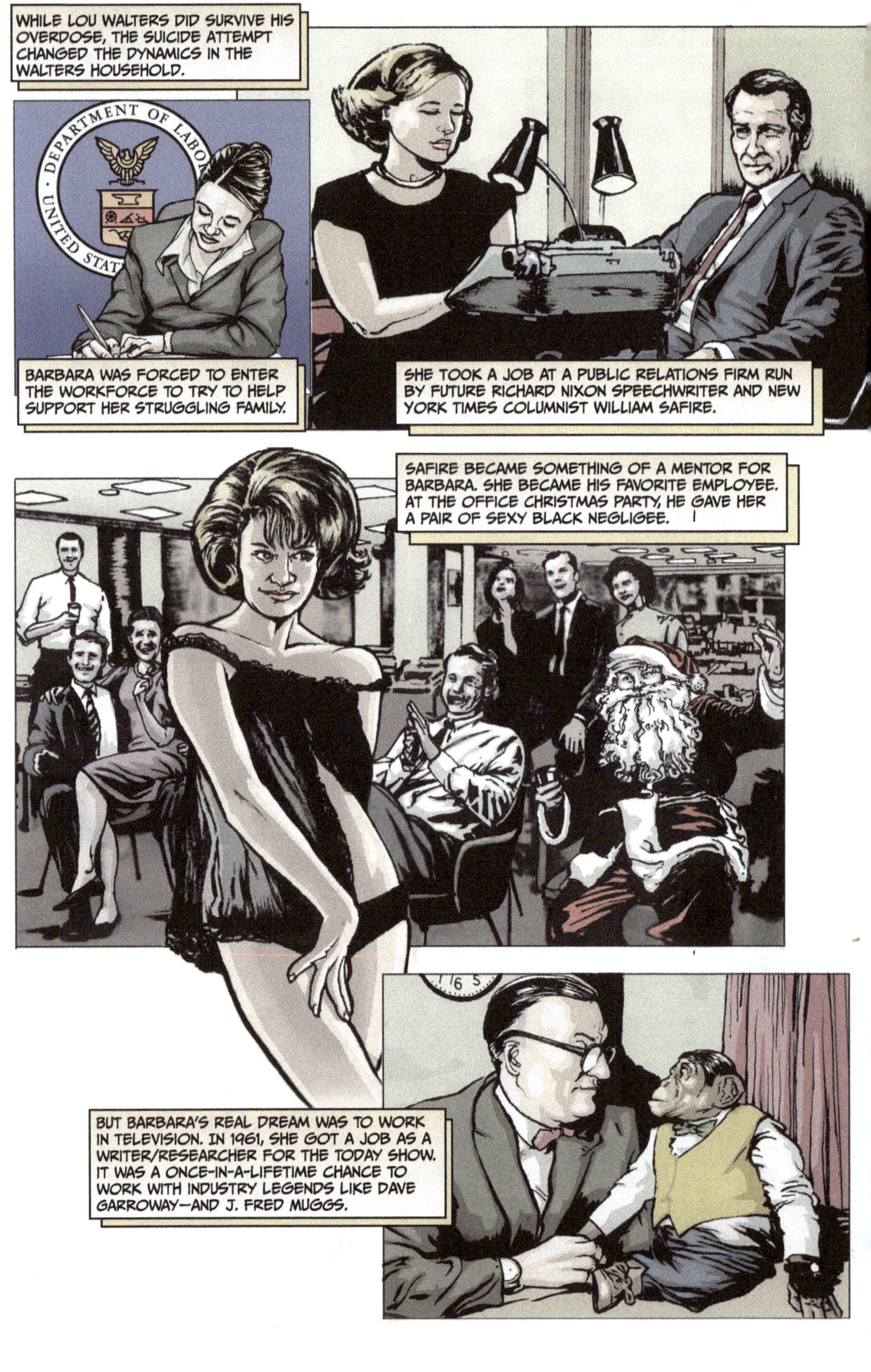

WHILE LOU WALTERS DID SURVIVE HIS OVERDOSE, THE SUICIDE ATTEMPT CHANGED THE DYNAMICS IN THE WALTERS HOUSEHOLD.

BARBARA WAS FORCED TO ENTER THE WORKFORCE TO TRY TO HELP SUPPORT HER STRUGGLING FAMILY.

SHE TOOK A JOB AT A PUBLIC RELATIONS FIRM RUN BY FUTURE RICHARD NIXON SPEECHWRITER AND NEW YORK TIMES COLUMNIST WILLIAM SAFIRE.

SAFIRE BECAME SOMETHING OF A MENTOR FOR BARBARA. SHE BECAME HIS FAVORITE EMPLOYEE. AT THE OFFICE CHRISTMAS PARTY, HE GAVE HER A PAIR OF SEXY BLACK NEGLIGEE.

BUT BARBARA'S REAL DREAM WAS TO WORK IN TELEVISION. IN 1961, SHE GOT A JOB AS A WRITER/RESEARCHER FOR THE TODAY SHOW. IT WAS A ONCE-IN-A-LIFETIME CHANCE TO WORK WITH INDUSTRY LEGENDS LIKE DAVE GARROWAY—AND J. FRED MUGGS.

AROUND THIS TIME, BARBARA FOUND LOVE FOR THE SECOND TIME IN THE ARMS OF THEATRICAL PRODUCER LEE GUBER.

THEY WERE MARRIED ON DECEMBER 8, 1963.

THE NEXT YEAR, BARBARA MOVED IN FRONT OF THE CAMERA WHEN SHE WAS PROMOTED TO THE POSITION OF "TODAY GIRL"—AN OLD, SEXIST TERM FOR A FEMALE CORRESPONDENT.

HER DUTIES WEREN'T GLAMOROUS. SHE WAS MOSTLY ASSIGNED HUMAN INTEREST STORIES, LIKE REPORTING FROM A CONVENT ON THE SECRET LIFE OF NUNS.

IT WAS AN EARLY EXAMPLE OF THE KIND OF SEXISM BARBARA WOULD HAVE TO DEAL WITH THROUGHOUT HER CAREER. STILL, SHE PRESSED ON...

SHE SCORED A MAJOR COUP FOR THE TODAY SHOW WHEN SHE TRAVELED TO INDIA TO INTERVIEW THE DAUGHTER OF THE PRIME MINISTER, INDIRA GANDHI.

SHE DEVELOPED A REPUTATION AS AN INTERVIEWER OF CELEBRITIES. HER NOTABLE "GETS" INCLUDED JUDY GARLAND, PRINCESS GRACE, AND TRUMAN CAPOTE.

WAY FROM THE CAMERAS, REASONER REFUSED TO EVEN SPEAK TO BARBARA.

TAXI!

ON CAMERA, HE COULD BARELY CONTAIN HIS DISDAIN FOR HIS NEW FEMALE PARTNER.

I'VE KEPT TIME ON YOUR STORIES AND MINE TONIGHT. YOU OWE ME FOUR MINUTES.

AT TIMES, HE OPENLY MOCKED HER.

YOU KNOW HARRY, HENRY KISSINGER MAY NOT LOOK THE TYPE, BUT HE IS CONSIDERED TO BE RATHER A SEX SYMBOL IN WASHINGTON.

YOU'D KNOW MORE ABOUT THAT THAN I WOULD, BARBARA.

BARBARA PUT UP WITH THIS ABUSIVE PROFESSIONAL RELATIONSHIP FOR TWO YEARS. IT DIDN'T HELP THAT RATINGS FOR THE NEWSCAST TANKED.

EVER ONE TO TAKE SIDES, BARBARA INTERVIEWED BOTH PARTICIPANTS IN THE BILL CLINTON/MONICA LEWINSKY SEX SCANDAL.

ALL THOSE BIG "GETS" MADE BARBARA A HUGE RATINGS DRAW. DURING THE 1980s, SHE WAS TWICE NAMED IN GALLUP POLLS AS ONE OF THE MOST RESPECTED WOMEN IN AMERICA.

ON THE HOME FRONT, BARBARA MARRIED AGAIN, IN 1986, TO LORIMAR TELEVISION CEO MERV ADELSON.

THE THIRD TIME WASN'T THE CHARM, HOWEVER. THEY DIVORCED SIX YEARS LATER.

WHILE SHE WAS COURTING MERV, HER SISTER JACKIE SUCCUMBED TO OVARIAN CANCER— A DEVASTATING LOSS THAT STILL HAUNTS BARBARA TO THIS DAY.

OUTSPOKEN LIBERAL ROSIE O'DONNELL'S ARRIVAL IN 2006 WAS A CONSTANT SOURCE OF IRRITATION FOR BARBARA.

BUSH LIED! THOUSANDS DIED!

CHRISTIANITY IS AS MUCH OF A THREAT AS ISLAMIC TERRORISM!

O'DONNELL FEUDED CONSTANTLY WITH CONSERVATIVE ELISABETH HASSELBECK—AND EVERYONE ELSE WHO DISAGREED WITH HER.

YOU'RE A FAT UGLY COW!

YOU'RE AN ORANGE-HAIRED PIG!

WHEN THE MORBIDLY OBESE O'DONNELL PICKED A PUBLIC FIGHT WITH THE EQUALLY ODD-LOOKING DONALD TRUMP, THAT WAS THE LAST STRAW. THE CONTROVERSY BROUGHT BUZZ, BUT WAY TOO MANY HEADACHES.

BARBARA FORCED ROSIE OUT, REPLACING HER WITH THE LESS CONFRONTATIONAL WHOOPI GOLDBERG. IT WAS A SIGNAL TO THE WORLD THAT THE EXECUTIVE PRODUCER WAS STILL VERY MUCH IN CHARGE.

WITH GOLDBERG AND SHERRI SHEPHERD NOW IN PLACE, THE VIEW WENT BACK TO BEING WHAT IT ONCE WAS: A FORUM FOR SPIRITED—AND RESPECTFUL—DISCUSSION OF ISSUES AND EVENTS OF THE DAY.

#ERASEHATE WITH THE MATTHEW SHEPARD FOUNDATION

With your donated dollars and volunteer hours, we work tirelessly to erase hate from every corner of America through our programs.

SPEAKING ENGAGEMENTS
Since Matt's death in 1998, Judy and Dennis have been determined to prevent others from similar tragedies. By sharing their story, they are able to carry on Matt's legacy.

HATE CRIMES REPORTING
Our work to improve reporting includes conducting trainings for law enforcement agencies, building relationships between community leaders and law enforcement, and developing policy reform in reporting practices.

LARAMIE PROJECT
MSF offers support to productions of The Laramie Project, which depicts the events leading up to and after Matt's murder. It remains one of the most performed plays in America.

MATTHEW'S PLACE
MatthewsPlace.com is a blog designed to provide young LGBTQ+ people with an outlet for their voices. From finance to health to love and dating, and everything in between, our writers contribute excellent material.

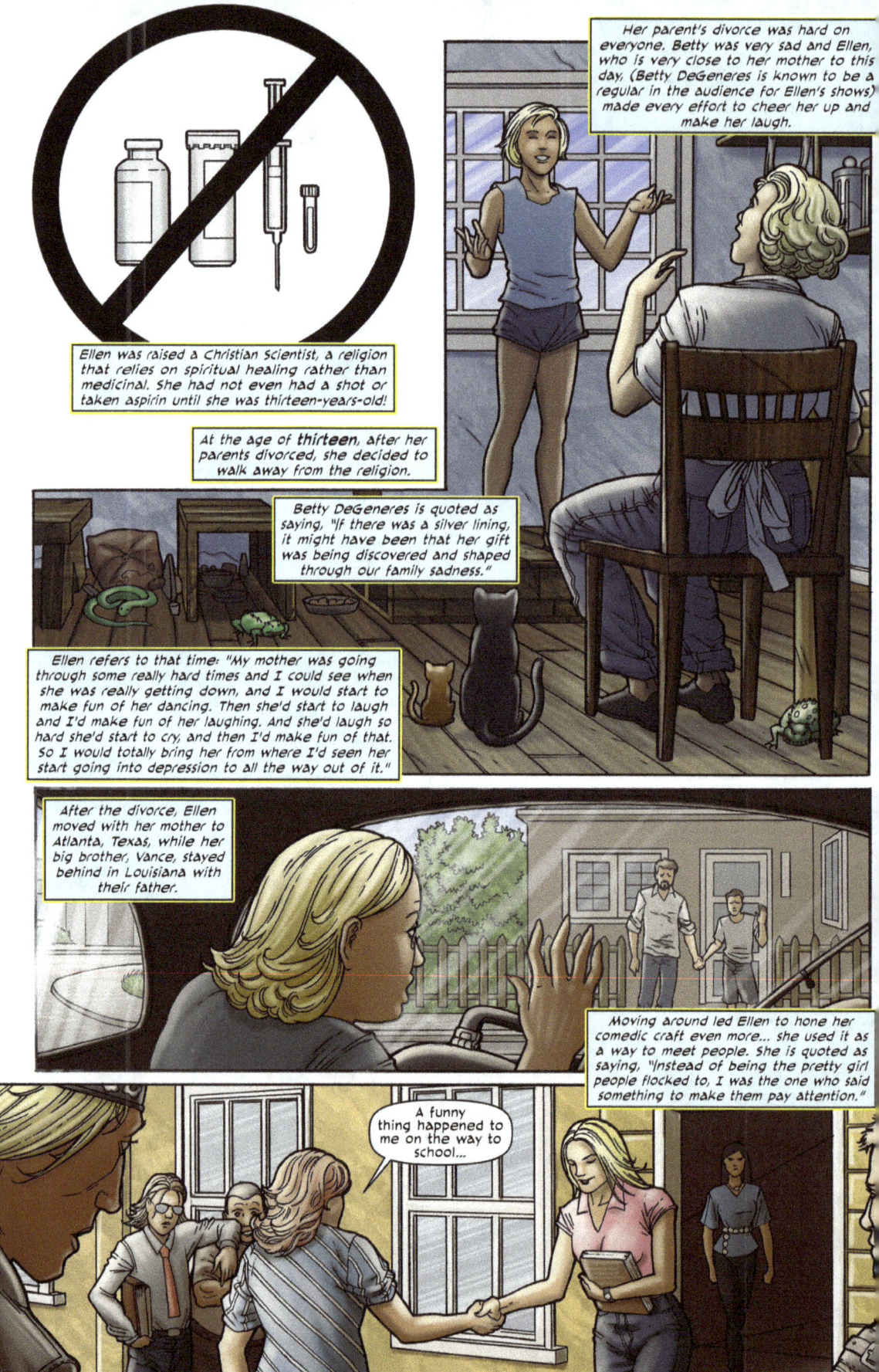

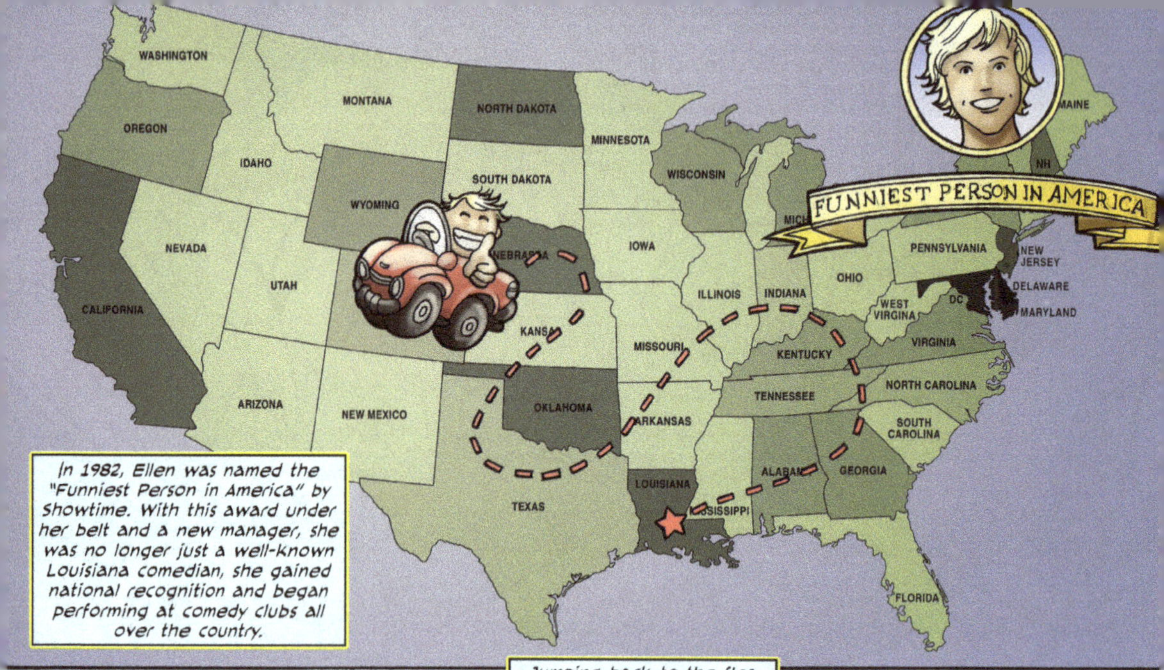

In 1982, Ellen was named the "Funniest Person in America" by Showtime. With this award under her belt and a new manager, she was no longer just a well-known Louisiana comedian, she gained national recognition and began performing at comedy clubs all over the country.

Jumping back to the flea infested mattress, Ellen had a premonition after writing her "Phone Call to God."

"I'm going to do this on Johnny Carson, and I'm going to get called over to the couch, and I'll be the first woman in history ever to get called over."

In 1985, Ellen made the move to Los Angeles. A move that would prove to pay off.

Ellen continued her club tours around the world, including some HBO specials, and more appearances on *The Tonight Show*. In 1991 she earned one of the many awards to come in her career, "Best Female Stand-up Comic" at the *American Comedy Awards*.

With her name on the rise, it was time to try her hand at television acting. She appeared in two short-lived sit-coms, "*Open House*" and "*Laurie Hill*", before landing a role in an ensemble cast show called "*These Friends of Mine*". In the show, Ellen played a bookstore employee (soon to be owner) named Ellen Morgan. It premiered on ABC in 1994.

The first season's ratings were mediocre, but people responded well to Ellen's character and the network saw her potential. So for the second season the network decided to make her character the lead and to change the show's name to "*Ellen*".

"*Ellen*" provided a venue for Ellen to display her comedic talents both verbally and physically. Her physical comedy was reminiscent of **Lucille Ball** and **Laverne & Shirley**.

Ellen, already defined as a tomboy, soon made a rare appearance in a dress. She co-hosted the 1994 Emmy's with Patricia Richardson from *Home Improvement*. As quoted by her mother, Betty DeGeneres, "The shocker, at least to those of us who know her well, was the sight of Ellen striding elegantly across the stage in a long, low-cut black gown." Ellen does **not** like to wear dresses.

I can't blame her...

During this time, Ellen decided to try her hand at writing and movies.

She wrote her first book, "*My Point... And I Do Have One*" which debuted at #1 on the New York Times Bestseller list. She would later write another book called "*The Funny Thing Is...*" which would also hit the New York Times Bestseller list in it's debut.

Ellen was less successful with her first starring role in the film, "*Mr. Wrong*". Critics saw the potential in her but criticized the overall movie.

"Mr. Wrong" may have been more successful if it was titled "Mrs. Wrong", as the world was about to find out.

On April 14, 1997, Ellen DeGeneres came out as a lesbian on the cover of Time magazine.

I'm gay.

And not only was Ellen DeGeneres coming out of the closet, her sitcom character Ellen Morgan was as well... making Ellen the first openly gay lead in a television show. Ellen made history once again!

On April 30, 1997, the 2-part episode, code-named "The Puppy Episode", was watched by over 42 million people... which would have been the equivalent of an opening weekend movie box office of $280 million!

Ellen and her writing staff won an Emmy for best comedy writing for the "The Puppy Episode".

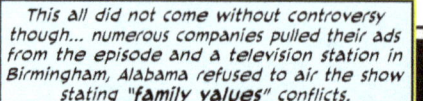

A couple of years after the cancellation of Ellen's sitcom, her much publicized, three-and-a-half year relationship with actress Anne Heche also came to an end in August of 2000.

The two had originally met at a post-Oscars "Vanity Fair" party in 1997 and immediately felt a connection.

Ellen gave the sitcom world one more try with **The Ellen Show** in 2001 but ratings for the show never quite took off and it was cancelled after 3 months.

"Everyone *hates* me now."

After the cancellation of both her shows and the end of her relationship, Ellen went through a challenging time.

She felt like her career was over.

She also felt that her overly-publicized relationship with Anne Heche might have ostracized some of her loyal fans.

It wouldn't be long, however, before Ellen would make people smile and laugh again... at a time when they really needed it. America would entrust her with its pain.

Terror and tragedy struck America on September 11th, 2001. For months after, people questioned if life would ever be the same again.

The Emmy Awards were originally set to air September 16th of that year. People questioned if it would be too insensitive to air a celebration given what the world was experiencing. The Emmys ended up being postponed twice after the tragedy.

"I guess this is *business casual*."

Finally, on November 4, 2001 Ellen DeGeneres hosted the 53rd Annual Emmy Awards.

"We're told to go on living our lives as usual, because to do otherwise is to let the terrorists win, and really, what would upset the Taliban more than a *gay woman* wearing a suit in front of a room full of *Jews*?"

The crowd roared with laughter and gave Ellen several standing ovations throughout the night. She took a sensitive yet clever approach that said it is ok to laugh again. She might have pulled from her past experience when she used to try to make her mom laugh after her parent's divorce.

Ellen wrapped her arms around the country and the country in return wrapped their arms back around her.

It was time for Act 2 in Ellen's life...

"I *like* where this is going. New beginnings make me want to dance!"

Next on Ellen's to do list, a critically acclaimed, highly-rated talk show. On September 8, 2003 *The Ellen DeGeneres Show* premiered.

"I'm so excited for you..."

"What's better than getting you *everyday*?!"

Jennifer Aniston, one of Ellen's good friends, was Ellen's first guest.

She greeted Ellen with a "Welcome" mat.

Ellen got the whole world dancing. At the top of every show, after her monologue, she dances her way through the aisles of her audience, dances over her coffee table and plops down into her chair.

She is also notorious for giving away generous gifts to her audience. Her "**12 Days of Giveaways**" during the holiday season is very much an audience favorite.

This was Ellen's first foray into the talk show world and it was a success. It proved to be the right venue for her to entertain people. Her show came on at a time when everyone from Sharon Osbourne to Rita Rudner had their own talk show.

Ellen's show stood out amongst the others, critics and fans loved her!

In the show's first season alone it received a record 12 Daytime Emmy nominations, winning 4 that year, including Outstanding Talk Show. Since then she has earned numerous Emmys for Outstanding Talk Show and Outstanding Host. As of this printing, the show has won 25 Daytime Emmy Awards!

On May 1, 2009 *The Ellen DeGeneres Show* celebrated its 1000th show... 1000 and growing.

"Nobody say a *word*!"

And let me tell you tickets are hard to come by to get into a show, I have been successful only once out of very many attempts... especially those "**12 Days of Giveaways**"!

In 2007, one of Ellen's childhood dreams came true... she hosted the 79th Annual Academy Awards!

She was only the second woman to host the Oscars solo, Whoopi Goldberg was the first, but Ellen was the first woman to host the show wearing pants.

Regis Philbin said after the ceremony, "I thought Ellen was great. The only complaint, not enough Ellen!"

On her talk show the next day, overwhelmed with emotion and tears, she expressed what an important moment that was in her life.

"It represented so many things to me. It represented that people believed in me, they took a chance on me to hold something like that together... I was scared to death."

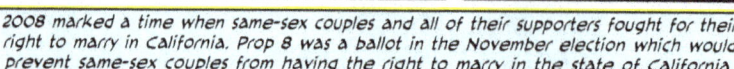

2008 marked a time when same-sex couples and all of their supporters fought for their right to marry in California. Prop 8 was a ballot in the November election which would prevent same-sex couples from having the right to marry in the state of California.

On November 4, 2008 Prop 8 passed and was put into effect the next day.

"Only marriage between a man and a woman is valid or recognized in California."

"Barack Obama has been elected as President of the United States!"

"Prop 8 has passed in the state of California."

"Watching the returns on election night was an amazing experience. Barack Obama is our new president. Change is here. I, like millions of Americans, felt like we had taken a giant step towards equality. We were watching history.

This morning, when it was clear that Proposition 8 had passed in California, I can't explain the feeling I had. I was saddened beyond belief. Here we just had a giant step toward equality and then on the very next day, we took a giant step away.

I believe one day a 'ban on gay marriage' will sound totally ridiculous. In the meantime, I will continue to speak out for equality for all of us."

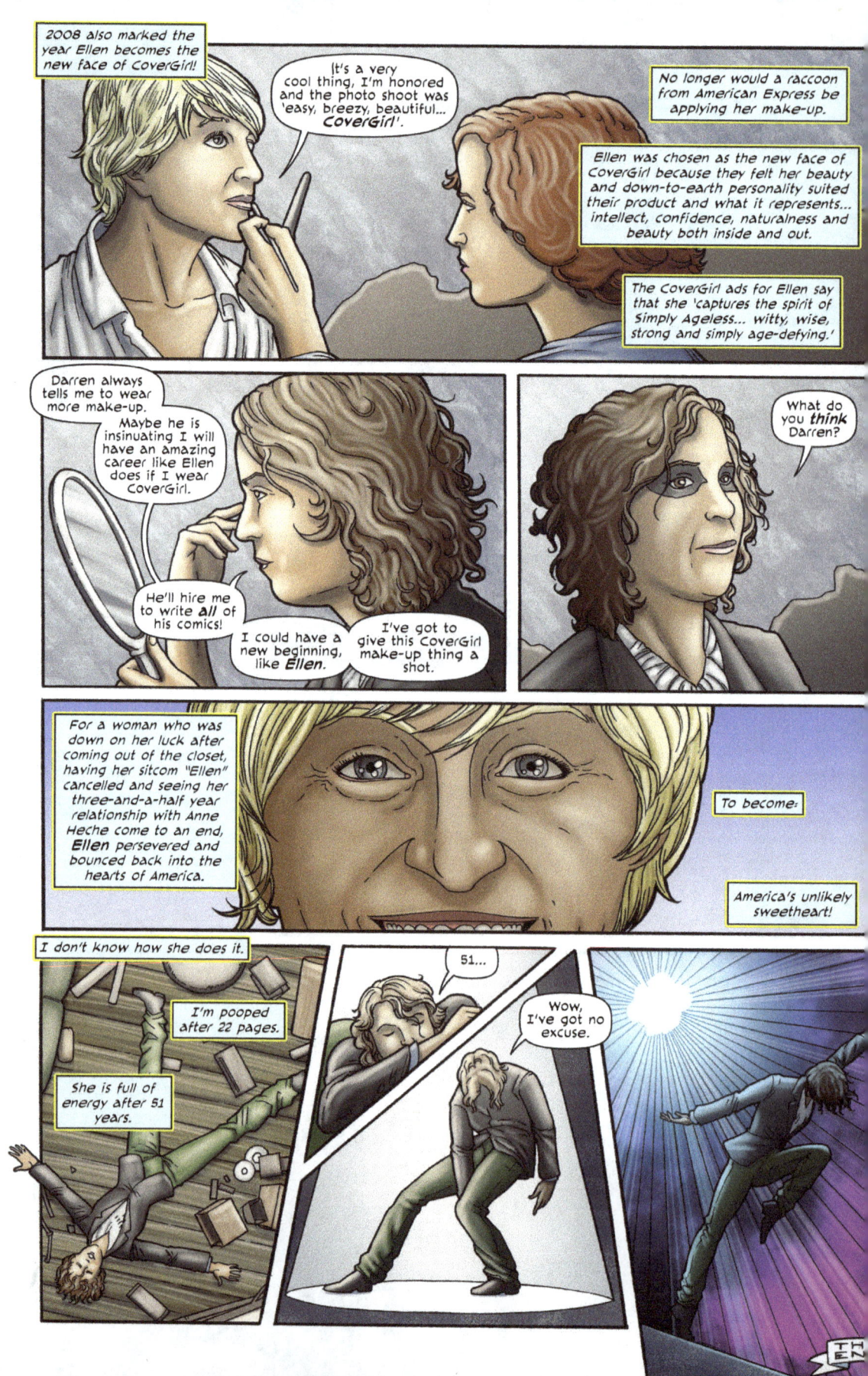

★FEMALE★FORCE★
Ellen DeGeneres

Sandra C. Ruckdeschel — Writer

Pedro Ponzo — Penciler

Kirtsy Swan — Colorist

Jaymes Reed — Letterer

Darren G. Davis — Graphics

Cover Vinnie Tartamella

Patrick Foster
Logo Design

Chad Jones
Production

Darren G. Davis
Publisher

Jason Schultz
Vice President

Lisa K. Brause
Entertainment Manager

Lisa Battan
Marketing Director

Janda Tithia
Coordinator

Scott Davis
Media Manager

Joshua LaBello
Creative Services

Vonnie Harris
New Business

Adam Ellis
Coordinator

www.bluewaterprod.com

FEMALE FORCE AND CONTENTS ARE COPYRIGHT © AND ™ DARREN G. DAVIS. ALL RIGHTS RESERVED. BLUEWATER COMICS IS COPYRIGHT © AND ™ DARREN G. DAVIS. ALL RIGHTS RESERVED. ANY REPRODUCTION OF THIS MATERIAL IS STRICTLY PROHIBITED IN ANY MEDIA FORM OTHER THAN FOR PROMOTIONAL PURPOSES UNLESS DARREN G. DAVIS OR BLUEWATER COMICS GIVES WRITTEN CONSENT. PRINTED IN USA www.bluewaterprod.com

Storm Entertainment's Full Digital Catalog On

Madefire

 Get it on Windows 10

 GET IT ON Google Play

 Download on the App Store

#ERASEHATE WITH THE MATTHEW SHEPARD FOUNDATION

With your donated dollars and volunteer hours, we work tirelessly to erase hate from every corner of America through our programs.

SPEAKING ENGAGEMENTS
Since Matt's death in 1998, Judy and Dennis have been determined to prevent others from similar tragedies. By sharing their story, they are able to carry on Matt's legacy.

HATE CRIMES REPORTING
Our work to improve reporting includes conducting trainings for law enforcement agencies, building relationships between community leaders and law enforcement, and developing policy reform in reporting practices.

LARAMIE PROJECT
MSF offers support to productions of The Laramie Project, which depicts the events leading up to and after Matt's murder. It remains one of the most performed plays in America.

MATTHEW'S PLACE
MatthewsPlace.com is a blog designed to provide young LGBTQ+ people with an outlet for their voices. From finance to health to love and dating, and everything in between, our writers contribute excellent material.

COMING NOV

THE MIS-ADVENTURES OF ADAM WEST
TRIBUTE

LEGENDS ARE FOREVER.

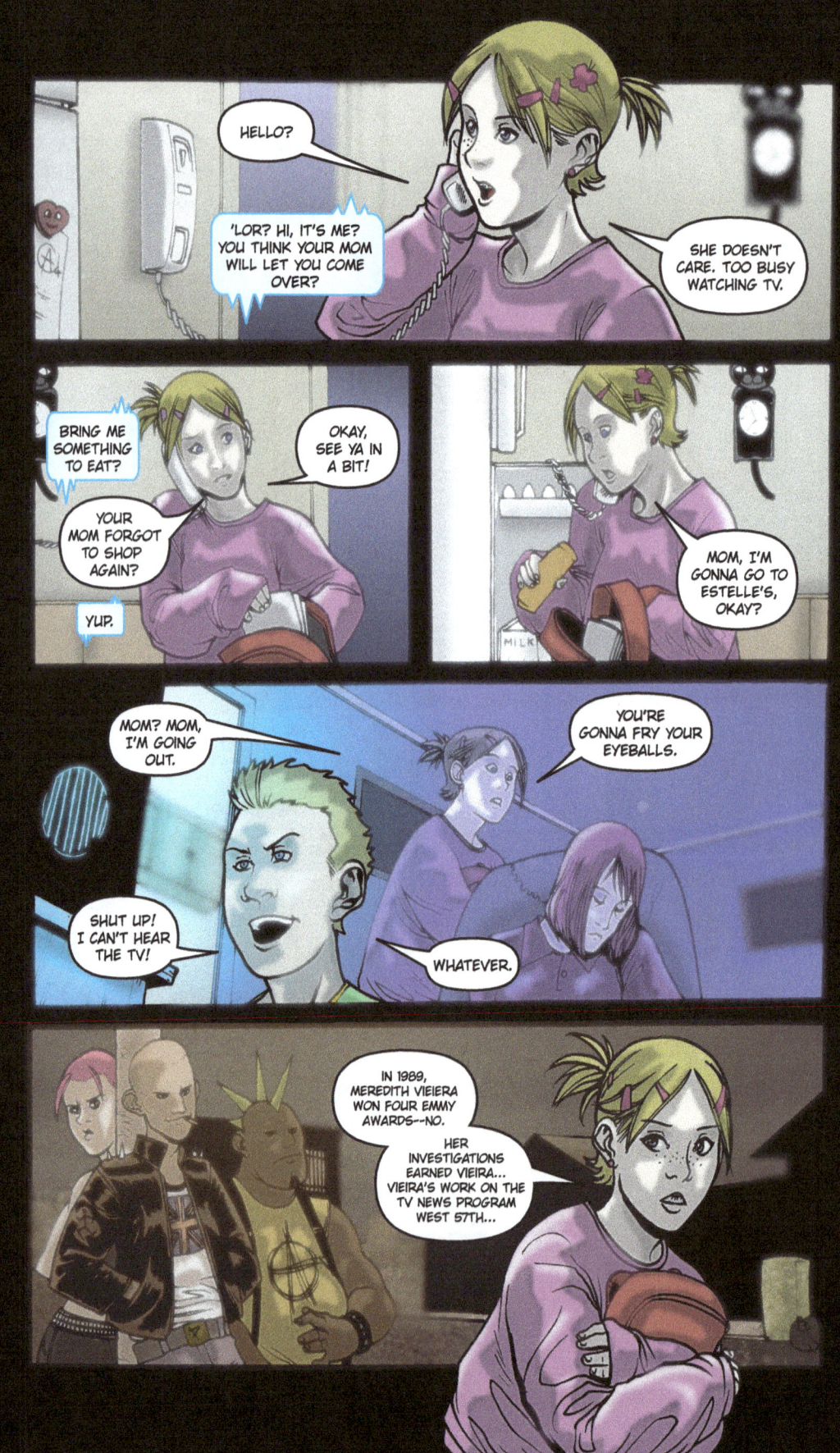

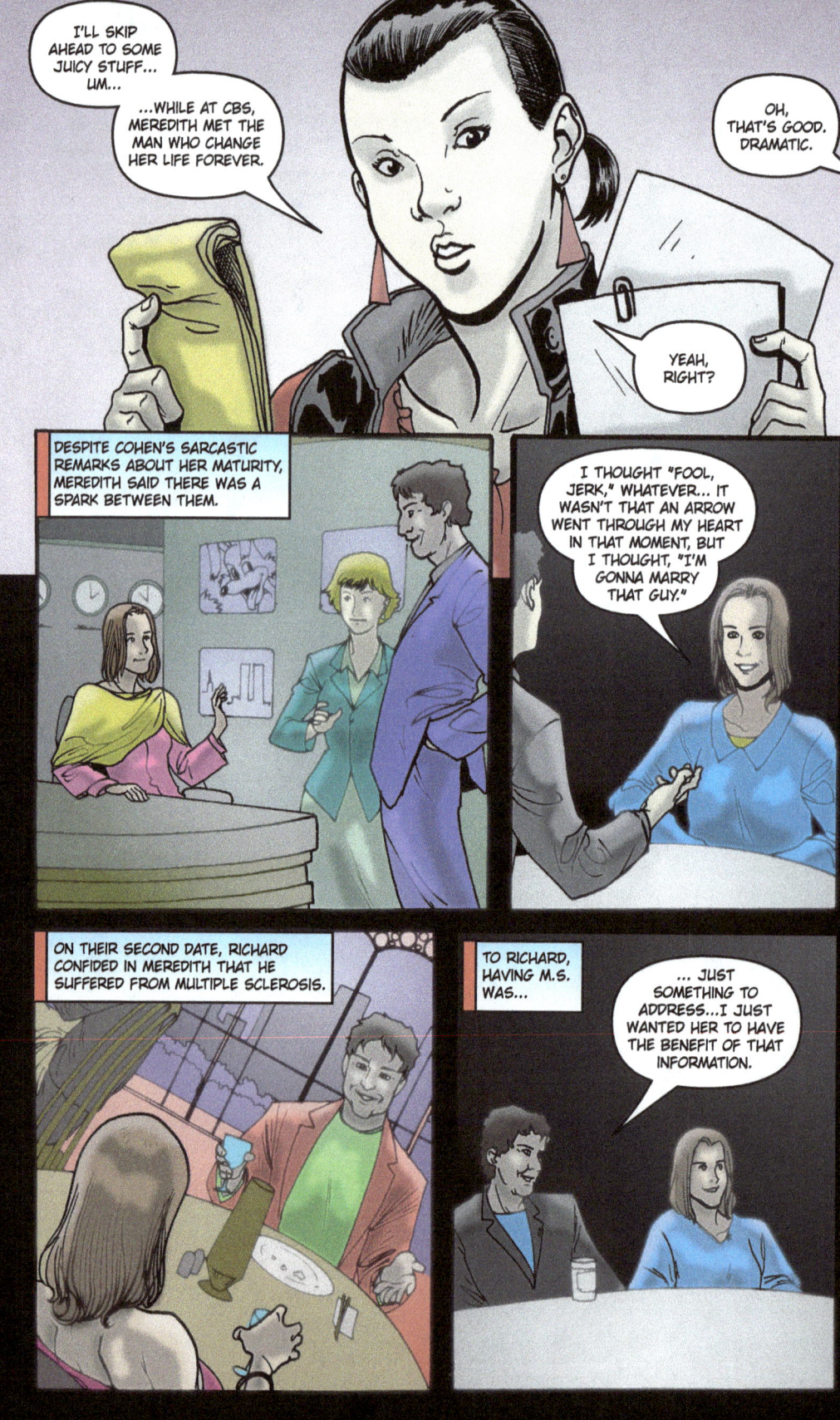

MEREDITH FOLLOWED UP HER MULTIPLE EMMY WINNING FOUR-YEAR RUN ON WEST 57TH BY BECOMING A CORRESPONDENT AND CO-EDITOR FOR 60 MINUTES.

AT 60 MINUTES, MEREDITH AGGRESSIVELY PURSUED SOME OF THE MOST IMPORTANT AND CONTROVERSIAL ISSUES OF THE DAY, EARNING RECOGNITION FOR HER "WARD 5A" STORY ON THE FIRST A.I.D.S. WARD IN SAN FRANCISCO...

...AND A FIFTH EMMY FOR HER STORY "THY BROTHER'S KEEPER" ABOUT CHRISTIANS WHO RISKED EVERYTHING TO SAVE THEIR JEWISH BROTHERS AND SISTERS DURING THE HOLOCAUST.

★ FEMALE ★ FORCE ★
Meredith Vieira

Brent Sprecher — Writer

Alex Lopez — Penciler

Willie Jimenez — Colorist

Wilson Ramos Jr. — Letterer

Darren G. Davis — Graphics

Darren G. Davis
Publisher

Jason Schultz
Vice President

Aha Maree
Creative Development

Crystal VanDiver
Director

Vinnie Tartamella
Cover

Chad Jones
Production

Janda Tithia
Coordinator

Scott Davis
Media Manager

Kim Sherman
Marketing Director

Vonnie Harris
New Business

Adam Ellis
Coordinator

www.bluewaterprod.com

FEMALE FORCE AND CONTENTS ARE COPYRIGHT © AND ™ DARREN G. DAVIS. ALL RIGHTS RESERVED. BLUEWATER COMICS IS COPYRIGHT © AND ™ DARREN G. DAVIS. ALL RIGHTS RESERVED. ANY REPRODUCTION OF THIS MATERIAL IS STRICTLY PROHIBITED IN ANY MEDIA FORM OTHER THAN FOR PROMOTIONAL PURPOSES UNLESS DARREN G. DAVIS OR BLUEWATER COMICS GIVES WRITTEN CONSENT.
www.bluewaterprod.com

#ERASEHATE WITH THE MATTHEW SHEPARD FOUNDATION

With your donated dollars and volunteer hours, we work tirelessly to erase hate from every corner of America through our programs.

SPEAKING ENGAGEMENTS
Since Matt's death in 1998, Judy and Dennis have been determined to prevent others from similar tragedies. By sharing their story, they are able to carry on Matt's legacy.

HATE CRIMES REPORTING
Our work to improve reporting includes conducting trainings for law enforcement agencies, building relationships between community leaders and law enforcement, and developing policy reform in reporting practices.

LARAMIE PROJECT
MSF offers support to productions of The Laramie Project, which depicts the events leading up to and after Matt's murder. It remains one of the most performed plays in America.

MATTHEW'S PLACE
MatthewsPlace.com is a blog designed to provide young LGBTQ+ people with an outlet for their voices. From finance to health to love and dating, and everything in between, our writers contribute excellent material.

WHILE SHE WAS A SENIOR IN HIGH SCHOOL, JOHN HEIDELBERG, A DISC JOCKEY AT WVOL RADIO, NOTICED OPRAH'S RESONANT AND ARTICULATE VOICE AND CONVINCED HER TO MAKE A DEMO TAPE.

SHE WAS HIRED TO DO NEWS REPORTS ON THE WEEKENDS AND AFTER SCHOOL FOR $100 PER WEEK.

OPRAH GRADUATED FROM EAST NASHVILLE HIGH SCHOOL WHERE SHE WAS VOTED 'MOST POPULAR GIRL'.

SHE WENT ON TO ATTEND TENNESSEE STATE UNIVERSITY WHERE SHE MAJORED IN SPEECH AND DRAMA.

OPRAH SEIZED THE OPPORTUNITY TO ENTER A LOCAL BEAUTY PAGEANT AND WENT ON TO WIN SEVERAL TITLES, INCLUDING: MISS FIRE PREVENTION, MISS BLACK NASHVILLE, AND MISS BLACK TENNESSEE.

1973.

SHE WAS HIRED BY WTVF-TV AND, AT 19, BECAME THE YOUNGEST PERSON AND THE FIRST AFRICAN AMERICAN TO ANCHOR THE NEWS IN NASHVILLE.

1976.

VERNON AND ZELMA PUT HER ON THE RIGHT PATH, BUT IT WAS TIME FOR OPRAH TO BECOME INDEPENDENT.

HIRED BY WJZ-TV, OPRAH MOVED TO BALTIMORE TO CO-HOST THE 6 O'CLOCK NEWS.

IT WAS AT WJZ-TV THAT OPRAH MET HER BEST FRIEND GAYLE KING, AN INTERN AT THE TIME.

SEEN AS TOO EMOTIONAL TO ANCHOR THE NEWS, OPRAH WAS 'DEMOTED' TO CO-HOST A DAYTIME TALK SHOW UNTIL HER CONTRACT RAN OUT.

ON 'PEOPLE ARE TALKING', SHE AND HER NEW CO-HOST RICHARD SHER'S ON-AIR CHEMISTRY LED THE SHOW TO BEAT OUT THE PHIL DONAHUE SHOW IN LOCAL MARKETS.

OPRAH FELT LIKE SHE FINALLY FOUND WHAT SHE WAS MEANT TO DO. BUT SHE KNEW THAT SHE COULDN'T REALLY BE HERSELF AS A CO-HOST.

WHEN SHE HEARD THAT A SHOW IN CHICAGO WAS LOOKING FOR A HOST, OPRAH SEIZED THE OPPORTUNITY AND BECAME OBSESSED WITH GETTING THE JOB.

IT'S ABOUT ACHIEVING YOUR DREAMS BUT NOT STOPPING THERE.

IT'S ABOUT FIGHTING FOR WHAT YOU BELIEVE IN.

AND LEAVING THE WORLD A BETTER PLACE THAN YOU FOUND IT.

IT'S ABOUT LEADING BY EXAMPLE.

AND WALKING THE TALK.

"AND REMIND YOURSELF THAT THIS VERY MOMENT..."

IT'S ABOUT NEVER FORGETTING WHERE YOU CAME FROM.

"IS THE ONLY ONE YOU KNOW YOU HAVE FOR SURE."

AND NEVER LOSING WHO YOU ARE.

*FEMALE * FORCE*
Oprah Winfrey

Joshua LaBello — Writer

Joshua LaBello — Penciler

Michelle Davies — Colorist

Wilson Ramos, Jr. — Letterer

Darren G. Davis — Graphics

Cover: Vinnie Tartamella
http://vinroc.deviantart.com/

Patrick Foster & Johnny Lowe
Logo Design

Chad Jones
Production

Darren G. Davis
Publisher

Jason Schultz
Vice President

Lisa K. Brause
Entertainment Manager

Katie Peterson
New Business

Janda Titha
Coordinator

Crystal Vandiver
Director

www.bluewaterprod.com

FEMALE FORCE AND CONTENTS ARE COPYRIGHT © AND ™ BLUEWATER PRODUCTIONS. ALL RIGHTS RESERVED. BLUEWATER COMICS IS COPYRIGHT © AND ™ DARREN G. DAVIS. ALL RIGHTS RESERVED. ANY REPRODUCTION OF THIS MATERIAL IS STRICTLY PROHIBITED IN ANY MEDIA FORM OTHER THAN FOR PROMOTIONAL PURPOSES UNLESS DARREN G. DAVIS OR BLUEWATER COMICS GIVES WRITTEN CONSENT. PRINTED IN THE USA www.bluewaterprod.com

#ERASEHATE WITH THE MATTHEW SHEPARD FOUNDATION

With your donated dollars and volunteer hours, we work tirelessly to erase hate from every corner of America through our programs.

SPEAKING ENGAGEMENTS

Since Matt's death in 1998, Judy and Dennis have been determined to prevent others from similar tragedies. By sharing their story, they are able to carry on Matt's legacy.

HATE CRIMES REPORTING

Our work to improve reporting includes conducting trainings for law enforcement agencies, building relationships between community leaders and law enforcement, and developing policy reform in reporting practices.

LARAMIE PROJECT

MSF offers support to productions of The Laramie Project, which depicts the events leading up to and after Matt's murder. It remains one of the most performed plays in America.

MATTHEW'S PLACE

MatthewsPlace.com is a blog designed to provide young LGBTQ+ people with an outlet for their voices. From finance to health to love and dating, and everything in between, our writers contribute excellent material.

www.ingramcontent.com/pod-product-compliance
Lightning Source LLC
Chambersburg PA
CBHW080445110426
42743CB00016B/3288